Fishing

Written by Sandra Iversen • Illustrated by Stephanie Walker

In the summer,
Mum likes to go fishing.

She takes her fishing line,
her hooks, her bait
and her hat.

Mum puts some bait on her hook.
She throws her line into the water and she waits.

She waits and she waits
and she waits.
At last, she feels the fish bite.
She pulls in her line.
No fish and no bait.

Mum puts some more bait on her hook.
She throws her line
into the water and she waits.
At last, she feels
the fish bite again.

She pulls on her line.
She pulls in a little crab.
"A little crab!" says Mum.
"We can't eat a little crab for dinner!"
She throws the little crab back into the water.

Mum puts some more bait on her hook.
She throws her line
into the water.
Then she waits and she waits
and she waits.
At last, she feels a big fish bite.

Mum pulls on her line.
She pulls and she pulls
and she pulls.
She pulls harder and harder
and harder.